Thanks

To Eliane, my wife whom I love tenderly, Séphora, Silas, Océane and to you Benjamin, little ray of sunshine, who have agreed to share this bohemian life with me; to my parents, always there when I need them; to Jean-Michel Rave, Jefko as well as the whole team of the Tournesol newspaper, who've saved my life; to Stéphane Columbo, my translator and friend of my youth; to Laurent Bachmann, my most faithful adviser, best galley companion and my personal computor technician; to Ingrid Schorro, Nicolas Mosimann, Béatrice Guerne, Heidi Arias, Lydia Fückiger, Mymi Garcias and all the others who I have forgotten who have translated into Spanish and German for me; to Augustin Bordet for this excellent translation into English, Esther and David Warnett, Regis Roulet who helped me get through the maze of administration, Bryce Wagner from ≪Creative Pool≫ (who has the most amazing goatee I have ever seen) and Rachel (thanks to the queen of England for having loaned her), all of whom have put the finishing touches to this work that you are reading; to Luc and Nicole Barder who have accompanied me a little way in the world of marketing; to Anne-Catherine and Iain Schneitter, who have allowed me to work in ≪La Ferme Imaginaire≫; to Sean Sauser and Rapael Augsberger, my devoted garage mechanics; to Luc Normandin, my crazy pastor and friend for having supported me; to those who were formerly in charge of ≪J'y crois≫ and the ≪Cave≫ for helping me to make myself; to Patrick and Lydie Vaucher, the champion dragon hunters; to Monique and Thierry Juvet from St-Loup as well as to Ohra my psychologist, to Tilly Gerber, Maja Belhil, Renate Normandin, my mother-in-law for having looked after such precious treasures and thus allowing me to devote myself to my work; to Patrick Tanner of the Mont-Soleil Festival; Manouk der Stepanion, my Hollywood friend; to Frédo Guerne, my facourite land-mine psychiatrist; to the team of ≪Oasis≫ and ≪Le Roc≫, my second family; to the tavern ≪Buffet de la Gare≫ where I often go and draw, to Ursula and Edward Schnegg for my first steps in a new life; to Juro Schnegg, for listening; to Margrit and Christophe (who left us too soon) Rüfenacht and Pierre Besançon, for their helping hand; to Fabio Gay and to her big heart, full of generosity; to Priscille Konrad, who gave me her car so that I could work; to Raynald Schnegg, my favourite cook; to Daniel Huguelet, who initiated me into the world of virtual reality; to Marc Jeanfavre, my favourite smurf and to his brother for his enthusiasm; to Christof Schnegg, uncontested master of controlled madness; to the team of the <<Phare>>, who have always supported me, to Marcello et Joel from be-TV, the semi-gods of the technological century, to Jacques Tschanz and his extraordinary wife Prescille, from the Salvation Army, to Didier Chassagnot, Hedi Brenner; Christian Willy (the pope of the French-speaking press), to Edmond Moret, Marcel Jeni, Rolf Honeisen, Erwin Buchmann, Peter Kipfer, Philippe Chevalley, Betty Lessart who published my very beginnings, and all the other newspapers who believed in my cartoon strips; to Paul Freiburghaus (male Mother Theresa); to Philippe Siraut, Lis and Kurt Buhlmann (the killer shark), Raphael Liechti, Dolores Sauser and David von Gunten (official graphic designer of the diary) who were mad enough to set foot into my universe, to Sara Kunz, the first secretary in the world ever to come and work here, to Lucia Amélia, sunshine from Brazil, to Vincent and Marie-Elise Fernandez and Sverker Blyth from Longwy; to Norma and Alejandro Escobedo from Mexico; to Gino the visionary and to Guillaume from ≪Chmurtz Animation≫; to Séverin Kézeu, inventor of AI and family; to Michel Balverne from CIJEM; to Eric Célérier and all his team from Top-Chrétien; to Paul Ettori, to Hélène Ha and Isabelle Lee from China; to Tony Collins who enabled the English edition of this book; to Henry Nissen from the newspaper ≪Udfordringen≫ my editor in Denmark, to Sam and Karin Barbey as well as Moïse and Marlene Ollivier for the translation; to Christian Stramm, to Heidi Lauber, Mad, Eric Long and all my other distributors across the universe; to Claudine Mevrat who has not yet perished in the jungle-depths of my accounts; to Pierre-Andre Perrin, to Bruno Jordi (the greatest printing legend in Europe) who had this book at heart; to all those who I've omitted to thank in my unpardonable ingratitude and to Jesus Christ, my best friend.

Alain Auderset is a professional illustrator based in Switzerland

www.auderset.com / Atelier Auderset / Mont-Soleil 22 / CH-2610 Saint-Imier / Suisse / Tel (++41) 32 941 51 19

Mill Hill, London & Grand Rapids, Michigan

French edition first published in Switzerland by the author in 2001.
English translation first published in the UK in 2006 by Monarch Books
(a publishing imprint of Lion Hudson plc), Mayfield House,
256 Banbury Road, Oxford OX2 7DH
Tel: +44 (0) 1865 302750 Fax: +44 (0) 1865 302757
Email: monarch@lionhudson.com
www.lionhudson.com

ISBN-13: 978 1 85424 755 1(UK)
ISBN-10: 1 85424 755 7 (UK)
ISBN-13: 978 0 8254 6113 2 (USA)
ISBN-10: 0 8254 6113 8 (USA)

Distributed by:
UK: Marston Book Services Ltd, PO Box 269, Abingdon,
Oxon, OX14 4YN
USA: Kregel Publications, PO Box 2607,
Grand Rapids, Michigan 49501.

British Library Cataloguing Data
A catalogue record for this book is available
from the British Library.

Printed in China.

1st step...

The Human Heart...

The next day...
Two days later:
They forecast rain again for tomorrow
What lousy weather we had yesterday!
A.AUDERSET©

Let's change this society!

hum...
hum...

Oh yeah, that's more urgent...
AA©

I don't give a rip, as long as it's not happening in my back yard
©A.AUDERSET

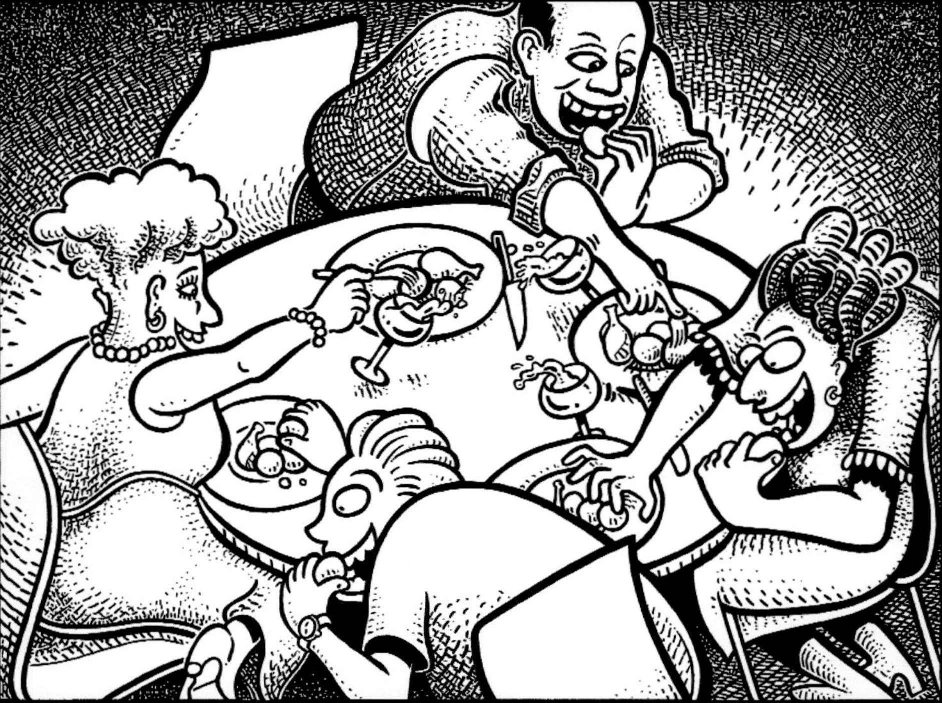

©A.AUDERSET

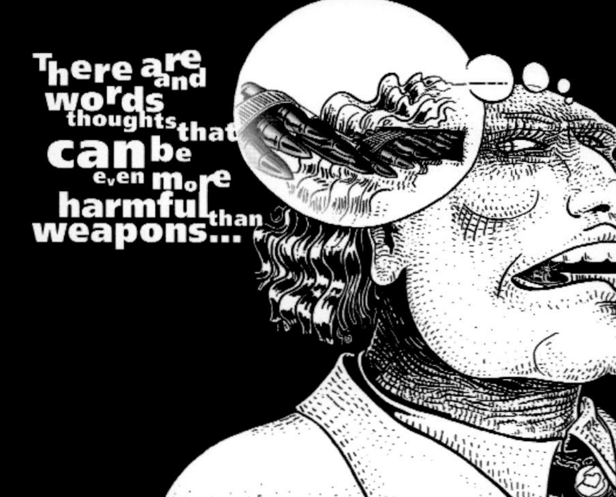

There are words and thoughts that can be even more harmful than weapons...

"Don't wait for a big occasion to give her flowers."

I love you
Like grown ups?
No, in my case, it's for real
www.auderset.com

So...?
You gonna keep it?
!!...
©A.AUDERSET
"Nothing's more important than good communication in a couple!"
Jasmine and I feel free to share anything
...so to speak...
A.AUDERSET©

This guy looks so superficial
MUM
A.AUDERSET©

Help me please
CHING! CHING!

?!
CHING! CHING!

How insensitive can you get?!
CHING! CHING!
DEAF GUITARIST - PLEASE HELP ME
A.AUDERSET©

ECSTASY?!¿
A.A.
Are you two... twins?!
Hic!
Uh, yeah
mm...
NO ALCOHOL
What on earth made you a wino and you an anti-booze freak?
I didn't have a choice with the kind of father I had!!
A. AUDERSET©

Drug addiction is not a game!!!

?!

D...Dad!
!?

Anywhere
ABC
DREAMS
NEW CIT
A.AUDERSET©

Wow! A magazine!
What Luck! Cool!
Free!
HOROSCOPES

Sign of the pigeon:
Today, you will have a crappy day.
HOROSCOPE

Scrape
Scrape
Scrape
A. AUDERSET©

A. AUDERSET ©

Man:
Master of the Universe!!
Another breakdown
Chug! Chug!
A.A.©

Don't ever say you're worthless...

"...Let no one glory in men..."

The Bible
1 Cor 3:21

2nd step...

Nature: random or created?

This stain is an accident... OK!

But what about this one!?!

If God existed, there would be no war!
You forget something Bob...
We're the ones droppi the bomb not Him!
AA©

God? huh!
...I only believe in what I can see!!

The path's not important! Being sincere is what matters!!
JESUS
A.AUDERSET©

Life is sometimes
like a soccer game...

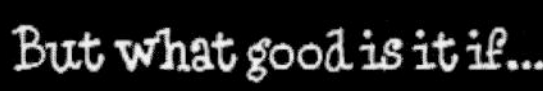
But what good is it if...

...there's no goal...?!?
A.AUDERSET©

!?
Give me a proof of God's existence...
A.AUDERSET©

MIRACLE!
THERE IS A GOD
who's doing something!
PLOP!
?!?
Bish!
Bash!
?!
GLL!
?!!
?!?
Hum... this is obviously not working!
Dad, I would like to teach love to those who will listen
duuuuuuh
duuuuuuh!
duuuuuuh!
©A.AUDERSET

The God of the Bible?
Too simplistic
THE BIBLE
Ha! Ha! Ha!
Are you kidding?
For starters, I don't like the term "GOD", I prefer to say: COSMIC POWER
I believe ...
it's some kind of energy ...
It's a light, our conscience within us...
I believe ...
it's everywhere, it's what brings nature to life...
I believe ...
...that all religions converge into one thing...
it's obvious
Trundle
The only thing that really matters is...
Love...
Love ...

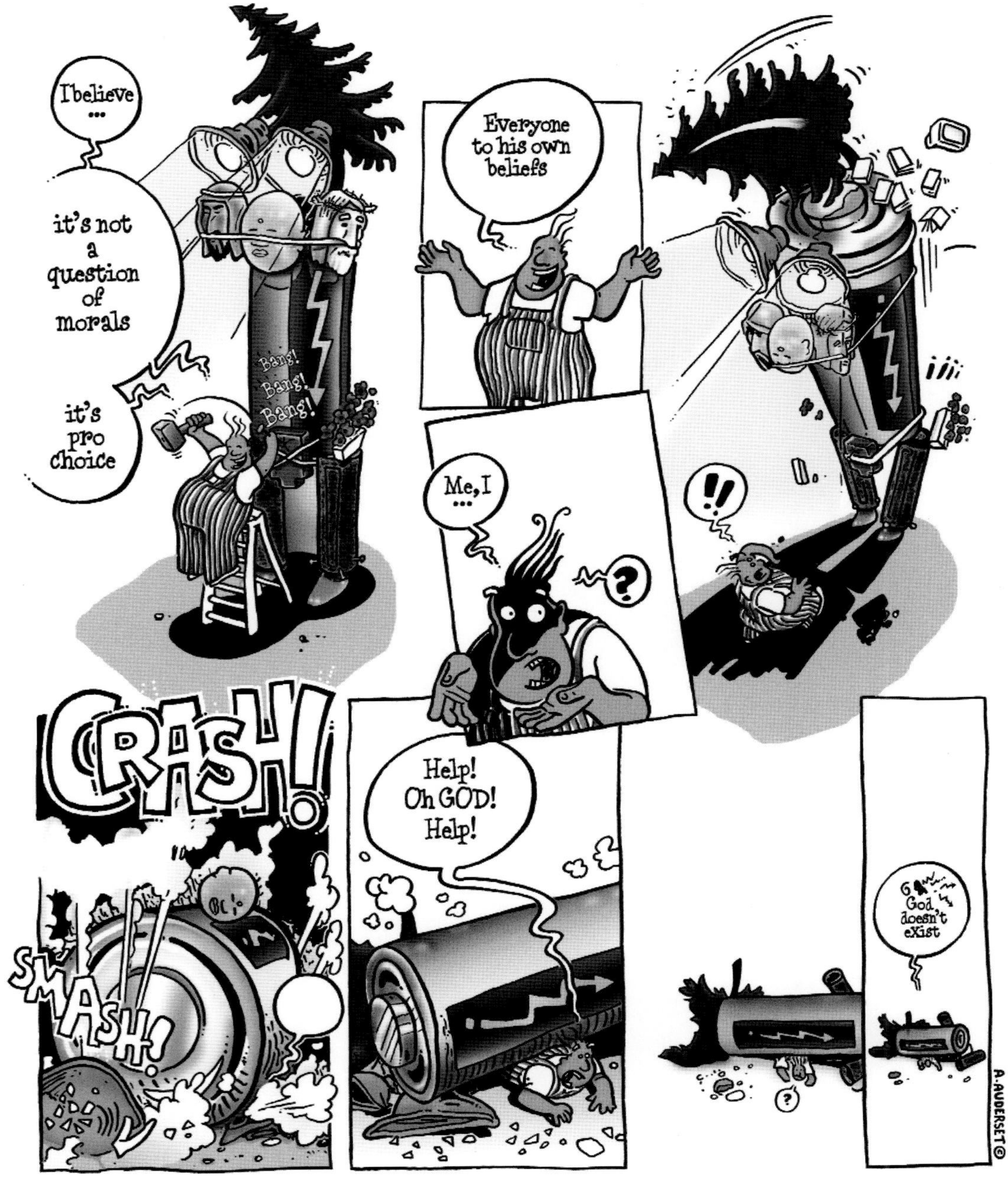

I believe ...

it's not a question of morals

it's pro choice

Bang! Bang! Bang!

Everyone to his own beliefs

Me, I ...

?

!!

CRASH!

SMASH!

Help! Oh GOD! Help!

God doesn't exist

?

A. AUDERSET©

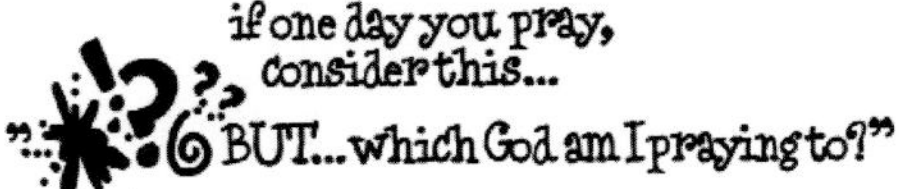

Where do we come from?
Who are we?
Why are we here?

?!?

ohhhh God,
why have you
left us without
any answers?!?

?!¿

THE BIBLE

CRASH!

A. AUDERSET ©

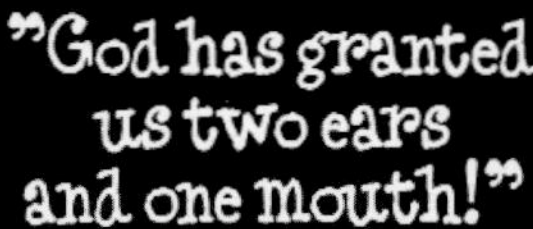

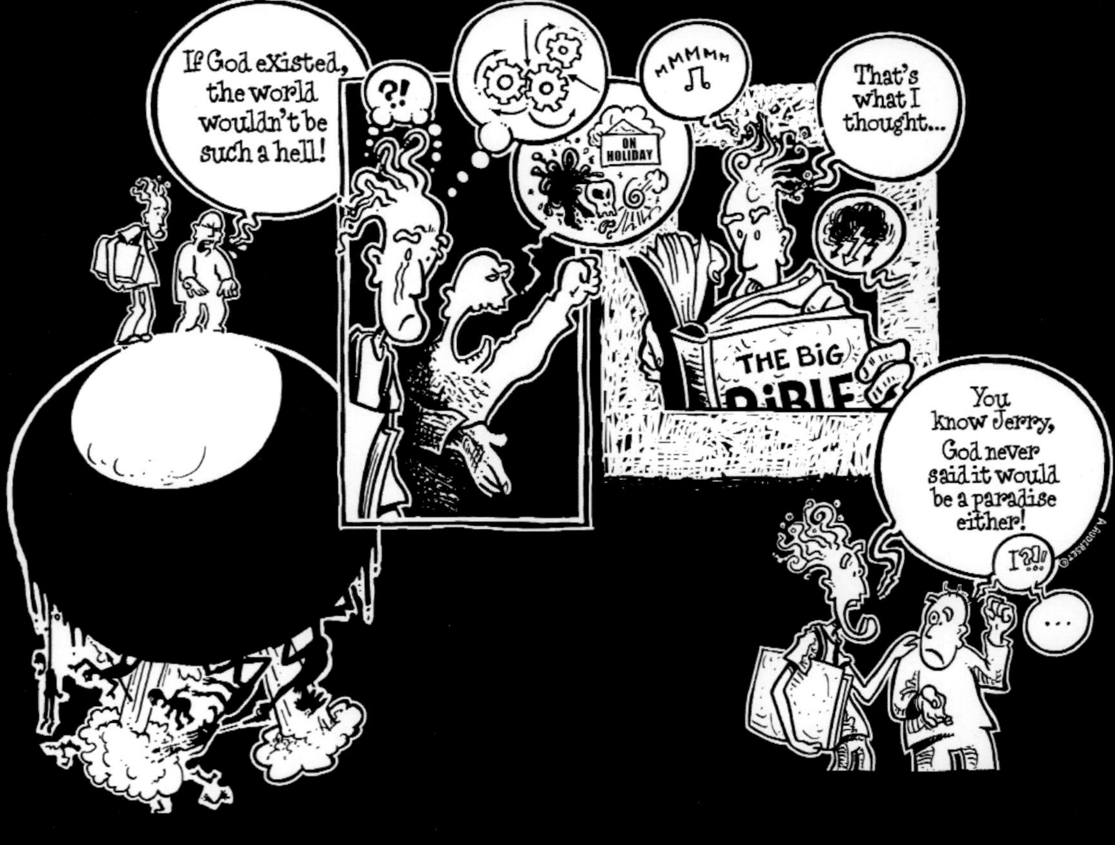

If God existed, the world wouldn't be such a hell!
?!
MMMMM
ON HOLIDAY
That's what I thought...
THE BIG
You know Jerry, God never said it would be a paradise either!
I?!!
...

All religions lead to Go...who?!!?

You can **lose** everything: your money!

your reputation!
Jerk!
your job!
?!?!
your loved ones!
your health!
I'm so fit!
Full of stamina!
THE BEST

your memory!

your friends!

your life!

your soul!!!

the only thing you can always Keep is God's love for us!

God has given us his most precious asset: **his son.**

"for God loved the world so much that he gave his only son
so that anyone who believes in him
shall not perish but have eternal life"
(the bible: john 3:16)

only you can **accept** this "gift",
by believing in him and by simply asking him
to come into your life and transform it.

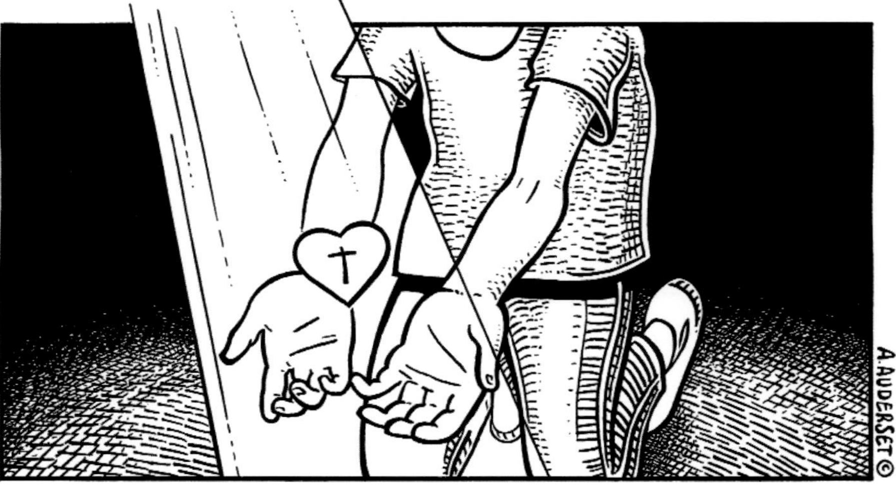

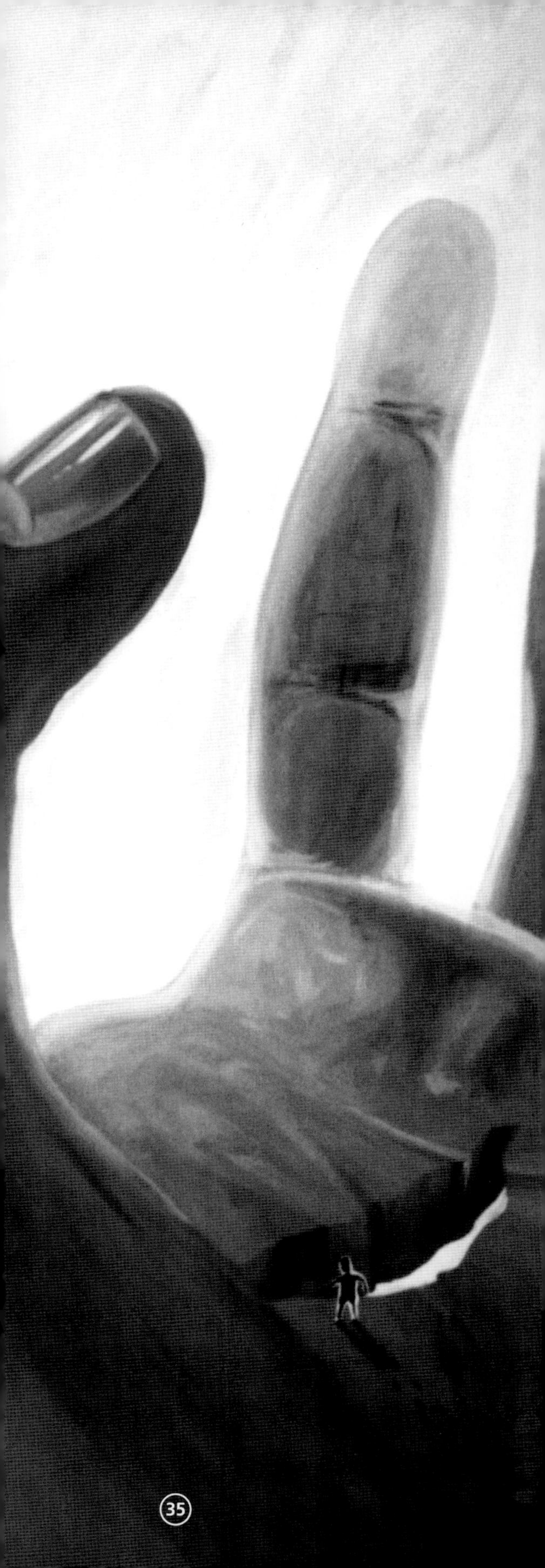

DANGER!
THE BIBLE
THIS BOOK CAN MAKE YOU HAPPY!!!
A.ANDERSEN©

Yeah...
Mmm! Crunch!
THE BIBLE
I admit it's kind of interesting... A little... boring at times...
a bit like my life...
PeterPrude begot straight-laced Simon who begot weeMary the latter begot some other guy, etc.
THE BIBLE
*NA: Personally, I find the concept of procreating rather eXciting!!!
How about using a little bit of the bottle?
The bottle? What's that all about?!! Oh yeah! The bottle!
*NA: Who the heck is talking in my comic strip?
Where is it?
ahhha.. there it is!
Rummage! Rummage!
Mmm... Not much left...
squish!
HA... after all, what do I risk?!
Plop!
A. AUDERSET ©
BOOM!

The Easter "hunt"...

There is something truly worth finding!

580–632
NOSTRADAMUS
MOHAMMED
BUDDHA
JESUS CHRIST
DANTA
AMI
UPADA
MAHATMA
GANDI
1869 — 19
KONG-TSEU
CONFUCIUS
L VI
— 1978
A.AUDERSET©

what is a man's life worth?!?
It depends on his purchasing power...
$
1000
3 camels for your wife
BANG!
BANG!
BANG
BANG!
oh...me...I'm not worth anything...I
NO!!!
don't ever say that, my friend, for you are invaluable, you have cost God his most precious asset:
his son!
A.AUDERSET©

But why does he love him so much?!?

...is it because he brings home money?

...or is it because he is so subservient?

...or is it because he is a little angel?

It's like God loves you

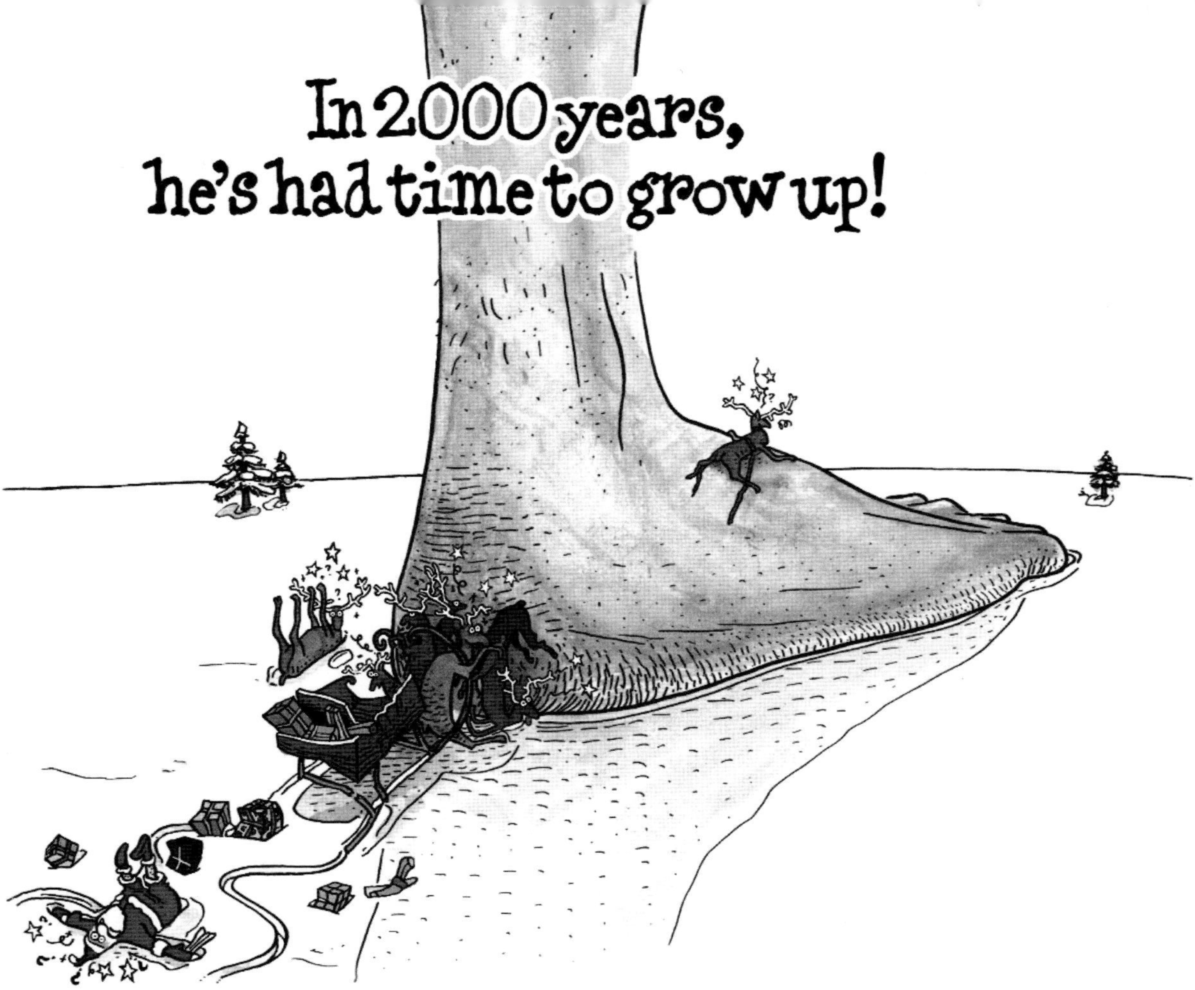

In 2000 years, he's had time to grow up!

The meaning of Christmas has been stolen!!

Willy, how do you do it...to be so cool??!
It's very simple, I know God
Hah?!
School of Theology
mystically mystic mysticism
BIBLE
GOD: Instruction Manual
Prayers in Cajun, Turkish and Ancient Latin
Who is Jesus Christ?
Hebrew -Ancient Greek - Swahili
how to make the Christian faith boring
Do Angels suffer from constipation?
HOW TO BECOME A BISHOP IN 10 LESSONS
Do high altitude ants have a soul? By Pr. C.Valium
much later
Willy, now I know loads about God but I'm still not happy!
!?!
SALVATION ARMY
Kurt, you may know a lot of stuff about God,
but you still don't know Him!
I hope I'm aiming at the right cloud!
A.AUDERSET ©

Hey Kurt so you believe in "Little Jesus" right? Then tell me one thing... Is the story about Jonah and the giant fish true?...
Boo
I'll ask him in Heaven!
So you reckon Jonah's in "Heaven"?
Hi Hi Hi
Well if he isn't, you can ask him yourself!
Gulp!
Drawing: A. AUDERSET© Idea: MICHEL BEGUELIN

Hi Kevin!
?!!

?!

My name is Jesus, ...you know Kevin...

I know all about you... I really love you...

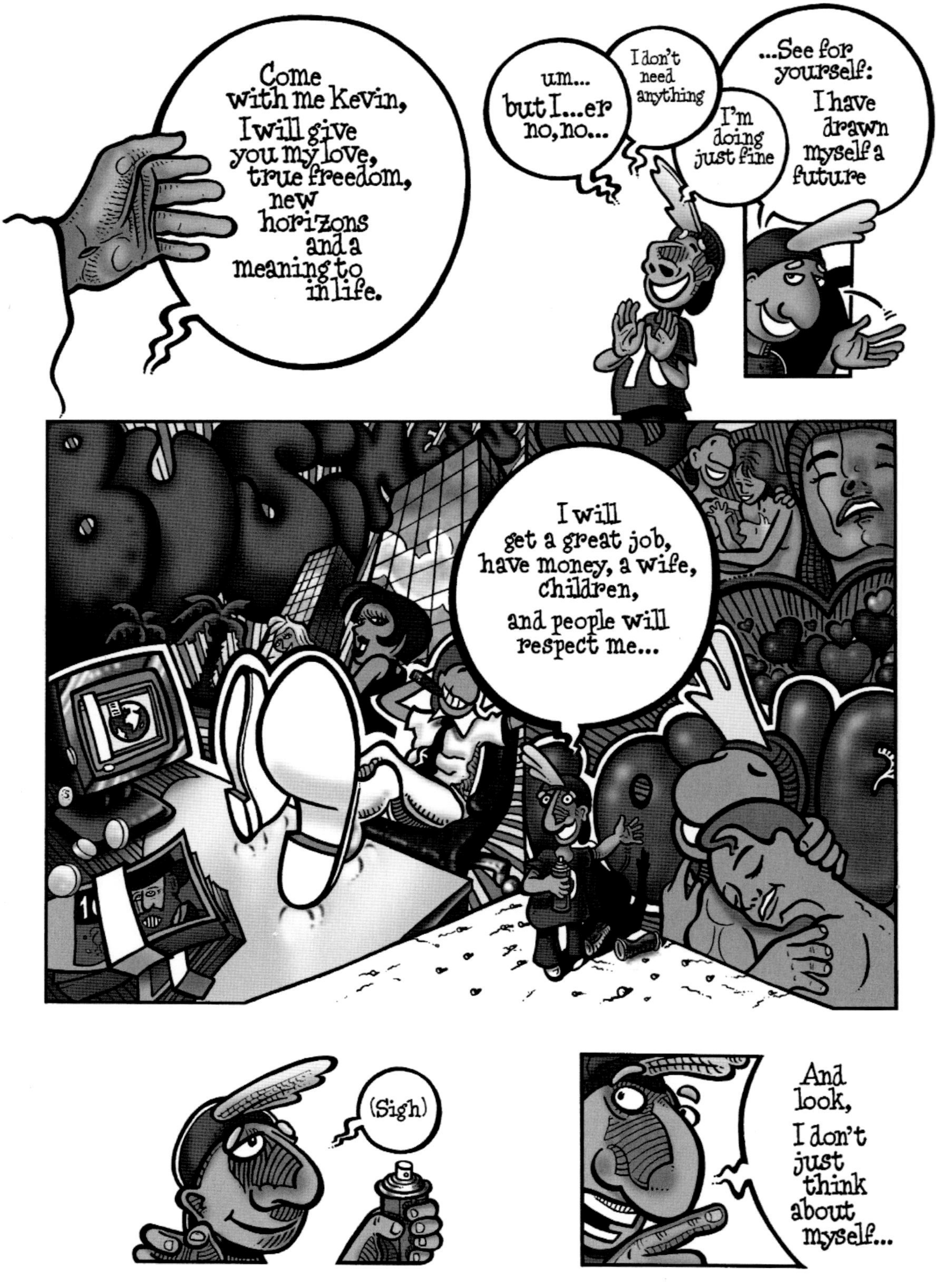

Come with me Kevin, I will give you my love, true freedom, new horizons and a meaning to in life.

um... but I...er no,no...

I don't need anything

I'm doing just fine

...See for yourself: I have drawn myself a future

I will get a great job, have money, a wife, children, and people will respect me...

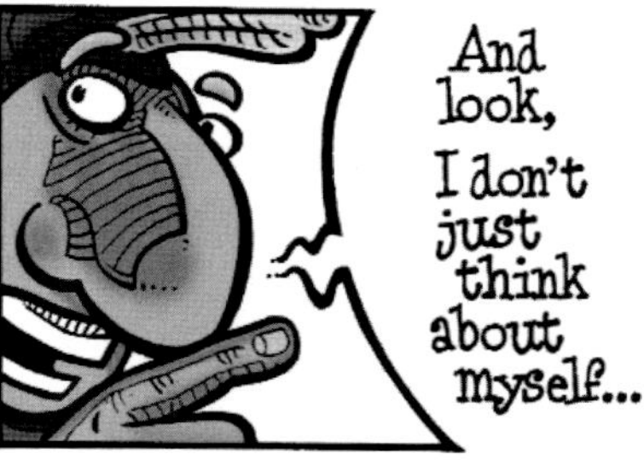

here's how I imagine the future, an era of peace, tolerance and progress, etc
And here you can see that I have some degree of spirituality... in my own way...
I throw everything together that suits me so I don't have question myself too much...
...I even have a little spot for the "Good Lord"...
Everything's cool, I forgive everything...
I figure we'll all go to heaven anyway
Well... that's about it ...
So, are you coming Kevin?

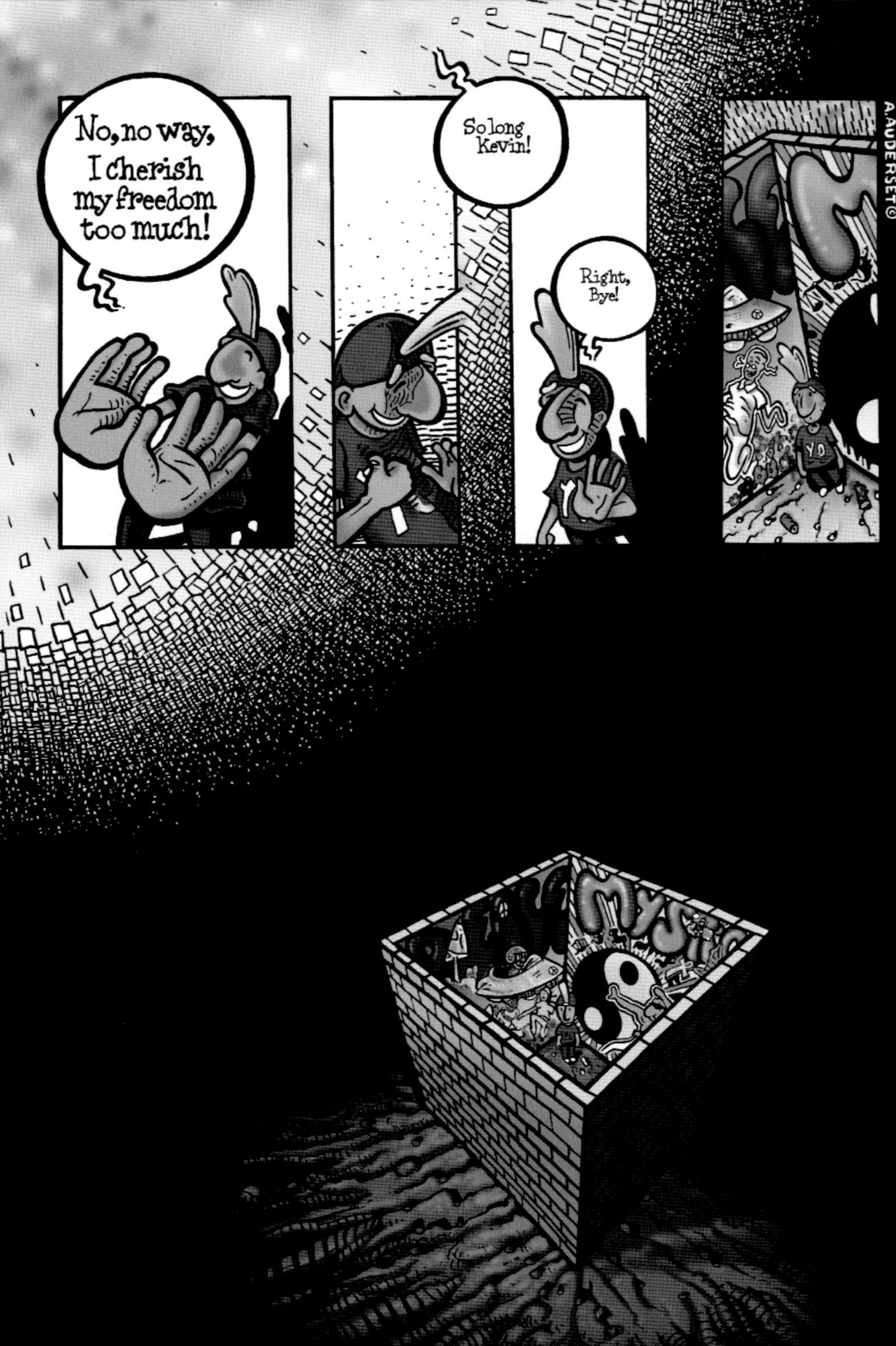

Jesus invites you to follow him too...

A.AUDERSET©

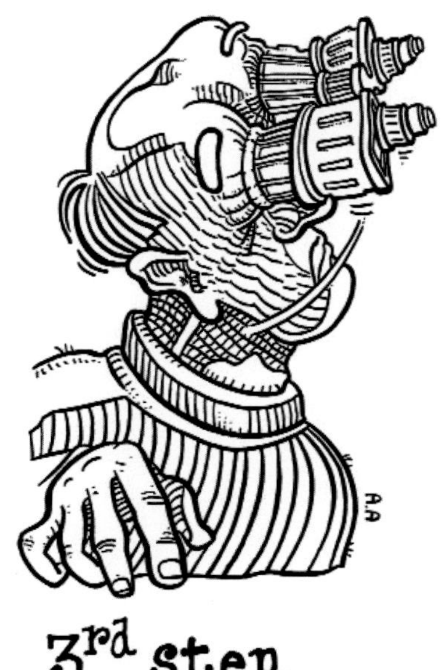

3rd step...

Non Practising Believer...

J. PETERSCHMITT + A. AUDERSET ©
Lord, is it true that, for you, 1 second is like 1000 years?!
mMmm (yes)
So a buck is like a million bucks, right?!
$
Rub Rub
Mmmm (yes)
So could you give me one of your little millions?
mMmm?
No problem my friend, just wait a second
...

"Hey mister, you're sitting on a bomb!"

Faced with this serious predicament, we can observe 3 possible reactions:

The non-believer's:

①

The believer's:

And the non-practising believer's:

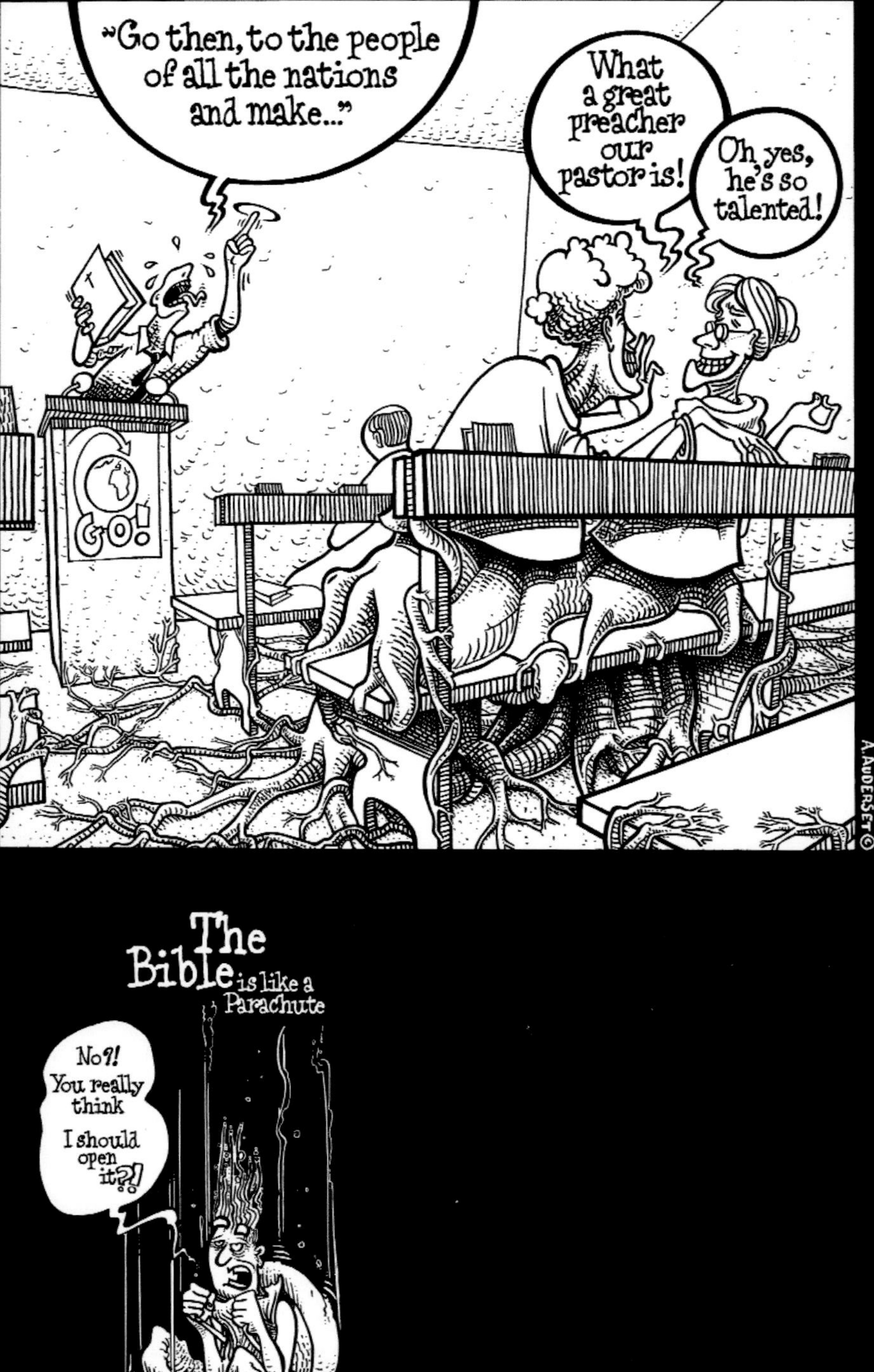

"Go then, to the people of all the nations and make..."
What a great preacher our pastor is!
Oh, yes, he's so talented!
GO!
A.AUDERSET©
The Bible is like a Parachute
No?! You really think I should open it?!
©AA

Is simply believing enough?
Of course I believe in the "Good Lord"!
GEORGIA
BEARS
Yo man, so do I
M...Me too...
©A.AUDERSET

I'm sorry Lord, but I ain't got time to pray, I'm too busy!
I'm sure you understand
Ah! I've got plenty of time...
I'll pray later...
I am on vacation after all!!!
VAMOS A LA PLAYA
FUN
DANGER
?!
?!
?!
FUN
DAN
Scrash!
Argh!
Help me Lord!
Get me out of here!
Our Father in Heaven...
A.AUDERSET©

What's wrong with this picture?

Answer:

"giving is giving, taking back is stealing"

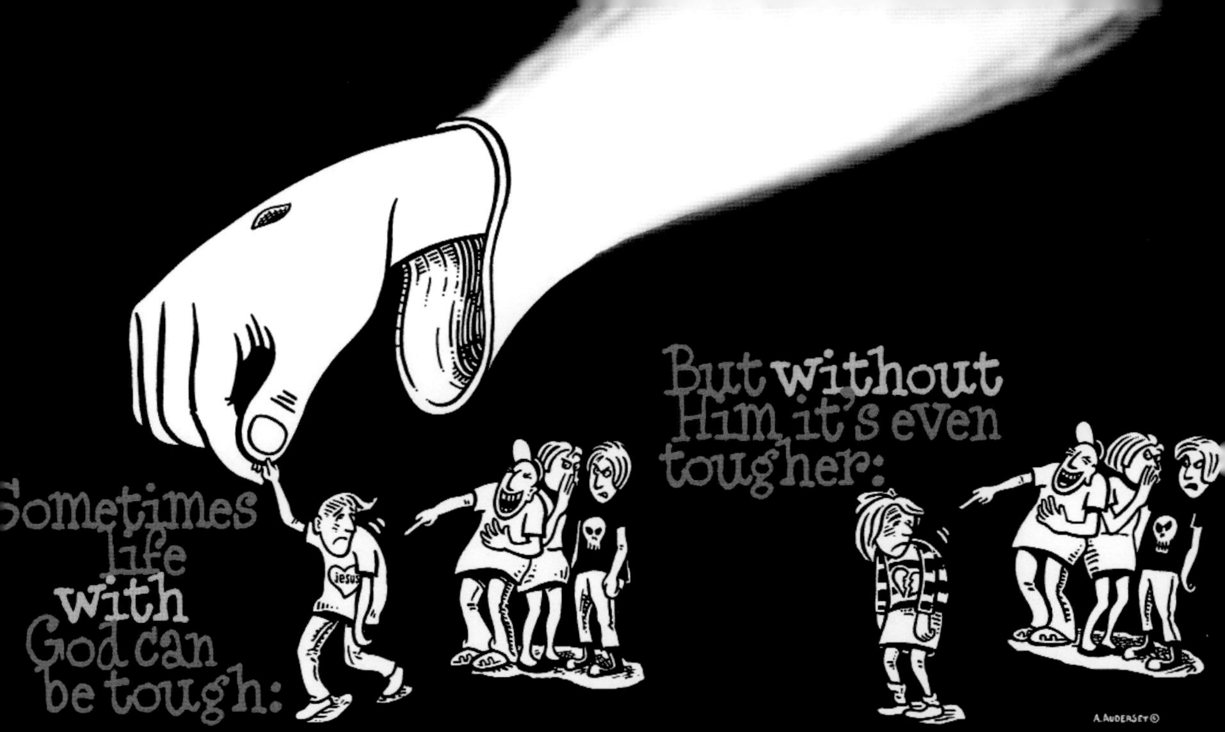

Sometimes life with God can be tough:

jesus

But without Him it's even tougher:

A. AUDERSET ©

Stop Compromise!

THE LAMB WHO THOUGHT HE COULD LIVE WITHOUT THE GOOD SHEPHERD:

The result of consuming too many sermons...

Some Bibles have great sentimental value:

Others are of immeasurable artistic and historical value:

But the most precious of all is the one that enriches your soul:

A.AUDERSET©

I believe in the existence of this glass, unfortunately, I'm not a practising drinker!!